AIR
RESCUE

BARRY D SMITH

AIR RESCUE

SAVING LIVES STATESIDE

Osprey Colour Series

Published in 1989 by Osprey Publishing
Limited
59 Grosvenor Street, London W1X 9DA

British Library Cataloguing in Publication
Data

Smith, Barry
    Air rescue
    1. North America. Rescue aircraft
    I. Title
    623.74'66

ISBN 0-85045-927-3

Editor Dennis Baldry
Designed by Vivienne Brar
Printed in Hong Kong

Front cover HH-65A Dolphin of
the US Coast Guard lowering a
rescue basket during a training
exercise with a rescue boat

Title pages A water rescue
performed by an HH-3E from the
129th ARRS based at Moffett Field,
California. The helicopter moves in
over the victim at ten knots and ten
feet. A pararescueman then jumps
into the water to secure the victim
to the rescue hoist. The
pararescueman is then hoisted
aboard the helicopter. The 129th is
a unit of the California Air National
Guard

A Sikorsky HH-3E Jolly Green
Giant and Lockheed HC-130P
Hercules of the USAF's 304th
Aerospace Rescue and Recovery
Squadron practise aerial refuelling
over British Columbia

This book is dedicated to the men and women who fly on rescue missions around the clock around the world

Acknowledgements

Throughout my travels to produce this book I encountered many people whose assistance was invaluable in obtaining information and photographic flights. From the US Coast Guard, I would like to thank Lt John Gaffney from the San Francisco Air Station, Lt Rick Gromlich from the San Diego Air Station, and Lt Ulrich from the Sacramento Air Station.

From the US Navy, I would like to thank Lt Bob Fallon at the US Navy News Desk in Washington, DC, Dennis McGrath and Lt Elizabeth Olmo at Lemoore Naval Air Station, California, and Teresa Bowman and Lt Cmdr Bruce Heywood at Fallon NAS, Nevada.

From the US Air Force, I would like to thank Captain Laughlin at the Office of Public Affairs in Washington, DC, Connie Rios and Captain Jim Kinzer at Kirtland AFB, New Mexico, and Karole Scott at the 939th Aerospace Rescue and Recovery Group, Portland, Oregon.

From the US Army, I would like to thank Lt Col John Chaplain at the Public Affairs Office in Washington, DC, Major Randy Schoel, Captain Mike Mokri, Captain Russell James, and 1st Lt Chris Landers at Fort Campbell, Kentucky.

From the Canadian Armed Forces, I would like to thank Lt Col M E Jay, Captain Rick Bedard, Captain Grant Griffith, and 1st Lt Marco Plasse at CAFB Comox, British Columbia.

I would also like to thank each and every crew that I flew with for their patience and enthusiasm for my project.

All the photographs in this book were taken with two Canon F-1 bodies and Canon lenses ranging in size from 17 mm to 200 mm. The film used was Kodak Kodachrome 25 and 64.

Introduction

The men and women who fly rescue missions are courageous, but it is a courage born of skill, training, and experience, not of ego or bravado. The crews go through extensive training in every phase of rescue and must maintain proficiency or lose their qualification to fly rescue missions. They must also have the courage to decline a mission when conditions are too hazardous.

Military rescue units tend to be small and close-knit. Strict observance of military customs and courtesies is usually waived. Respect is earned in these units, not commanded. Many times during the course of writing this book I encountered pilots and crewmembers who fought to get transferred to a rescue unit. Ask them why and you will get a variety of answers. One US Navy rescue pilot summed it up best when he told me:

> Other pilots ask me about it (rescue duty) and I tell them that they can go other places and do other things, but if they really want to have a good time flying and feel like they've really accomplishing something with their flying, rescue is a good place to go. After a rescue you look back and say to yourself, 'Hey, I hung it out a little bit, did a good job, got someone off the mountain, saved his life, and got the crew home safe.' It gives you a real sense of accomplishment. I'm on my second tour here and if I could get another I would take it.

Time and again, this is the spirit I encountered.

Barry D Smith
Morgan Hill, California
October 1988

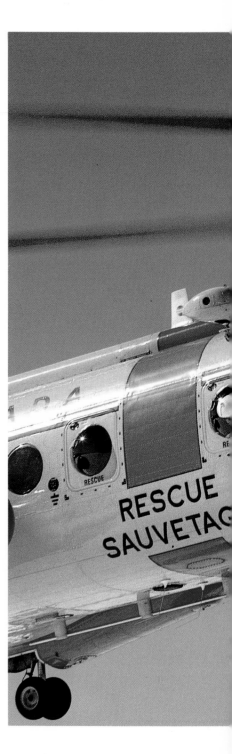

A Boeing-Vertol CH-113 Labrador of No 442 Sqn, Canadian Armed Forces, comes to the hover during a training mission from its home base at Comox, British Columbia. The Flight Engineer in the doorway is scanning below and behind the helicopter to guide the pilot and warn him of any obstacles

Contents

United States Coast Guard

Main picture The Sikorsky HH-3F Pelican medium range recovery helicopter has a watertight hull and can land on the water to pick up victims. The helicopter must be throughly rinsed with fresh water after the flight or corrosion will quickly set in. This Pelican is based at the US Coast Guard's San Francisco Air Station

Inset The crew of a 44-foot Motor Lifeboat prepares to take in the rescue basket lowered from an HH-3F. A crewman on the boat will ground the basket before touching it to discharge the static electricity. If this was not done, the shock could knock him overboard. Most hoist operations take place at about 35 feet. This allows the helicopter to sit on a cushion of air which reduces the workload on the engines and transmission

Main picture HH-3F over one of the many harbours in San Francisco Bay. Pleasure boating is very popular in this area and keeps the Coast Guard busy

Inset HH-3F over the rugged coast of northern California. Automobile accidents on remote roads are another type of call handled by Coast Guard helicopters

Left The HH-3F began operations with the Coast Guard in 1967. Some 40 machines were purchased to perform rescues up to 250 miles from base. Powered by a pair of General Electric T58 turboshafts, each rated at 1500 shp, the HH-3F can cruise at 150 mph

Below HH-3F and a Motor Lifeboat on an exercise off the California coast. An ideal hoisting situation has the boat steering about 30 degrees to the right of the wind and underway. This allows the helicopter to fly into the wind and properly position the hoist over the boat. The USCG uses a basket to hoist aboard uninjured survivors

A Lockheed HC-130H Hercules of the USCG undergoing maintenance at the Sacramento Air Station which is located on McClellan Air Force Base in central California. Sixteen new HC-130Hs were purchased to replace B, E, and early H model C-130s. They are based in California, Hawaii, Alaska, Florida and North Carolina. The HC-130H can carry 62,900 pounds of fuel. This can give an endurance of up to 13 hours, depending on the mission profile. To increase time on station, the crew can shut down two of the Allison T56 turboprop engines. In addition to SAR work, the Hercules perform fisheries patrols, drug enforcement surveillance, and iceberg patrols. They also haul pollution control equipment and disaster supplies over long distances. C-130s first entered USCG service in 1959

Main picture Dassault-Breguet HU-25A Falcon patrols off the coast of a southern California island. A typical mission will call for the Falcon to climb to 30,000 feet en route to the search area, descend to 500–1500 feet to search at 250 knots, and then climb back to altitude to return to base. The crew of an HU-25A consists of a pilot, copilot, dropmaster, scanner and radar/communications operator. A modified version of the Falcon 20 business jet, the HU-25A carries 10,000 pounds of fuel which gives it a four hour endurance plus a one hour reserve. The Falcon handles very well and is popular with its pilots. One said that it is 'very solid and smooth, like a well tuned sports car with tight shocks'. A total of 41 HU-25As serve with the USCG

Inset The crew of the Dolphin consists of a pilot, copilot and flight engineer. The flight engineer's seat moves from one side of the cabin to the other on rails in the floor. The large glazed area provides excellent visibility for the crew

Another French product, this Aérospatiale HH-65A Dolphin short range recovery helicopter is lowering a rescue basket to a 41 foot rescue boat. In order to allow the flight engineer to stand while operating the hoist, a hinged door in the top of the fuselage was placed next to it. The flight engineer is wearing a gunner's belt which allows him to lean way out of the helicopter without having to worry about falling out

The flight computer of the Dolphin can be coupled to the navigation system and perform a hands-off 50 foot hover over a specified point. The rotorhead of the Dolphin is also hi-tech; it contains 70 % fewer parts and weighs 60 % less than conventional rotorheads. It has no bearings and needs no lubrication. The rotor blades are manufactured using composite materials and have an infinite fatigue life

An HH-65 in the classic boat hoisting position which allows both the pilot and hoist operator to see the boat. The short mast on top of the rotorhead is the air data sensor. This device determines the direction and speed of the wind during flight, and the information it provides is used for navigation and autopilot functions

The instrument panel of the Dolphin is state of the art. There are few mechanical gauges. Video displays, digital readouts and vertical scale indicators are used to display information. The Dolphin is equipped with air-conditioning. It is not for the crew's benefit as much as it is used to cool the sensitive electronic systems. If the air-conditioning system is not working, the helicopter is not flown

Overleaf, left The hangar at the USCG's San Diego Air Station with three of the four HH-65As assigned there. Flotation bladders along the bottom edge of the fuselage automatically inflate if the Dolphin has to ditch. The Coast Guard ordered 96 Dolphins to replace the ageing HH-52A

20

Above HH-65A taking off from San Diego Air Station. Instead of a traditional tail rotor, the Dolphin has a shrouded fan which gives better crosswind control and uses less power. If the tail fan fails, the pilot can perform a running landing at 60 knots. In most other helicopters the pilot would have to resort to an emergency autorotation

Left The Dolphin's snout contains a sophisticated search and weather radar. Note the screens on the engine inlets to prevent the ingestion of foreign objects

United States Army

Inset First Lieutenant Chris Landers of D Company, 326th Medical Battalion, assigned to the 101st Airborne Division at Fort Campbell, Kentucky, at the controls of a medevac Sikorsky UH-60A Blackhawk helicopter of the US Army Medical Service Corps. Landers is wearing night vision goggles, as medevac helicopters must be able to perform their missions any time the troops are fighting, whether by day or night. All medevac helicopters use the call sign 'Dust Off', which orginated during the Vietnam War

Main picture The medevac helicopters at Fort Campbell keep a crew on alert at the airfield around the clock because of the large number of night flights on the ranges. The UH-60 is currently supplanting the UH-1H Huey, offering more power, more manoeuvrability, more cabin room and a much greater payload

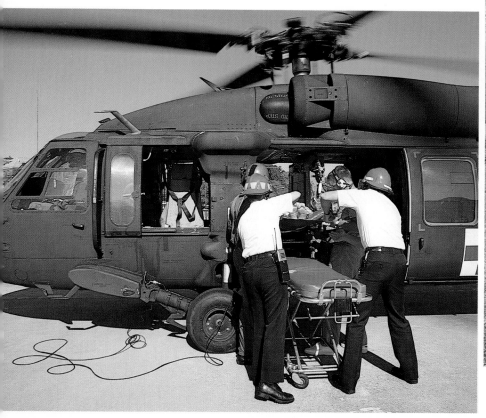
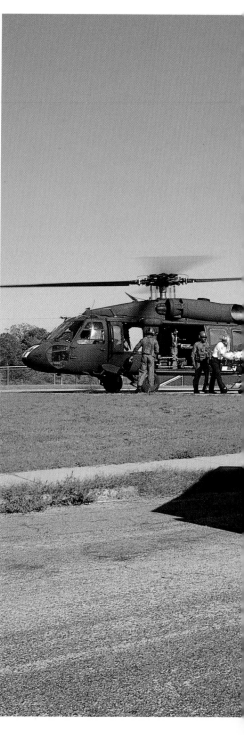

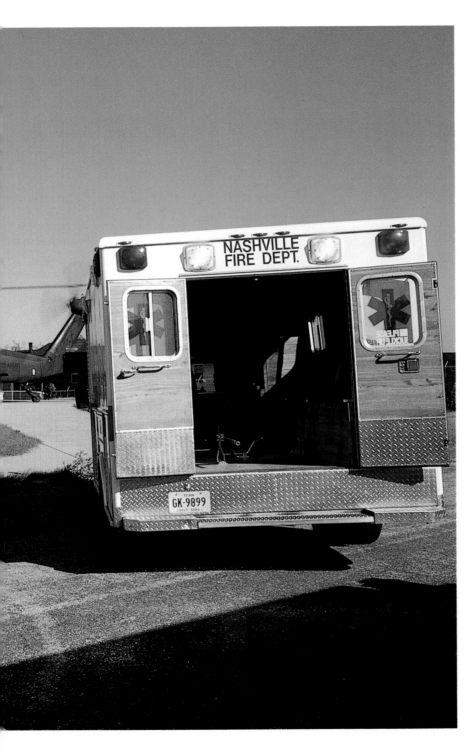

Top left The flight medic and hospital personnel roll a patient from an automobile accident out to a Blackhawk for evacuation from Blanchfield Army Hospital at Fort Campbell, Kentucky, to a specialist hospital in Nashville, Tennessee

Bottom left Paramedics from the Nashville Fire Department assist in unloading a patient they will transport to a local hospital from a helipad located at one of the paramedic stations

Left Nashville Fire Department paramedics wheel a patient to their ambulance after delivery by a Blackhawk from the 326th Med Bn

The stretchers are mounted on a revolving carousel in the Blackhawk's cabin. Three stretchers can be carried on each side but this leaves little room to work on the patients. Normally, only two stretchers are carried on each side

Patient carousel in the loading position: the platforms on which the upper stretchers sit can be lowered at one end so the stretcher doesn't have to be lifted so high when loaded

Inset The medevac helicopters at Fort Campbell are participants in the Military Assistance to Safety and Traffic (MAST) programme. This is a federal programme that uses military helicopters to respond to civilian emergencies to quickly transport the sick and injured to hospitals. Because of the rise in the number of specialized civilian medical helicopters, many military rescue units are now only called upon when a hoist is required.

Main picture The flight medic is using her feet to control the movement of the hoist cable and make sure it feeds correctly onto the spool. Although the medevac crews train regularly on hoist operations, they would rather land to pick up patients during combat. A helicopter in the hover is a sitting duck

Landing in thick grass requires a delicate touch by the pilot, who must be ready to add power pronto if the ground is uneven or he puts a wheel in a hole

Above The whole crew pays close attention when landing in a confined area. The crewmembers in the cabin are responsible for watching the tail and warning the pilot if there are any obstacles to the rear. Trees force helicopters to use more power in the hover in order to compensate for the loss of the cushion of air which is normally produced as touchdown nears. Designed to be crashworthy in the event of a mishap or enemy action, the landing gear of the Blackhawk can withstand 12G of vertical deceleration. The crew and passenger seats can absorb another 12G

Above Medevac UH-60 Blackhawk taking off from a meadow. Note the powerful downward deflection of the tailplane. This is to prevent the powerful downwash from pushing the tail down

Right 'Dust Off' Blackhawk sitting in a meadow at Fort Campbell during an exercise. The thick foliage and humid summer weather is reminiscent of South-East Asia

Above If a hoist operation is necessary in a combat setting, the crew will try to hover as close to the trees as possible to reduce exposure to hostile forces

United States Navy

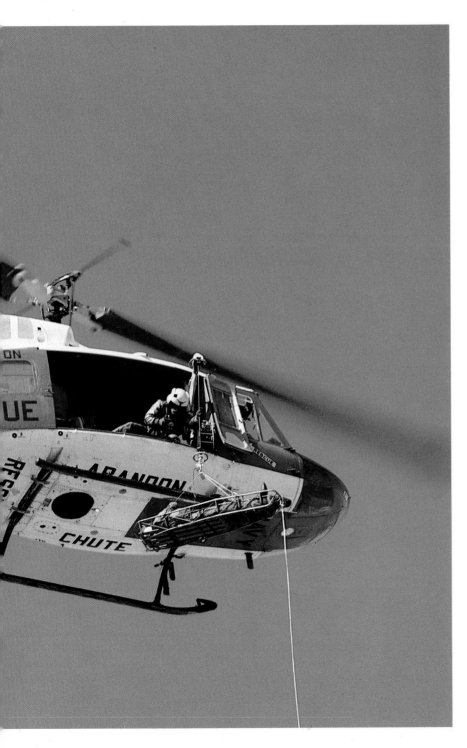

This sequence of photos shows a stokes litter being hoisted aboard a Bell UH-1N Twin Huey of the US Navy based at Fallon Naval Air Station in Nevada. The primary duty of the unit is to rescue downed crews operating in the extensive military range areas that surround the base. The line from the litter to the ground is used to steady it during ascent

Crewman set to rappel from a UH-1N based at Lemoore NAS in California, with a stokes litter. Rappelling gives the crewman control of his speed and allows for a faster descent than with the hoist. The rappel rope is kept in a bag on the crewman's side during the descent to keep from snagging any obstacles on the ground

The technique used when leaving the helicopter on a rappel. The crewman stands on the skid and slowly lets out line until his feet are above his head. He then begins a smooth, fairly rapid descent

Rappel from a Fallon NAS Twin Huey: a smooth exit keeps the helicopter from rocking back and forth, which can cause the rope to swing wildly. Once a pendulum action begins, it is very hard to stop and could slam the person on the rope into trees or rocks

During a short haul (also known as the fixed line fly-away), the pilot must make all changes in speed and direction very carefully. Any sudden movements will cause the people on the end of the rope to swing all over the place, possibly coming into contact with the ground in confined areas. A safety line is attached to the cable in case it should fail or it jams and has to be cut

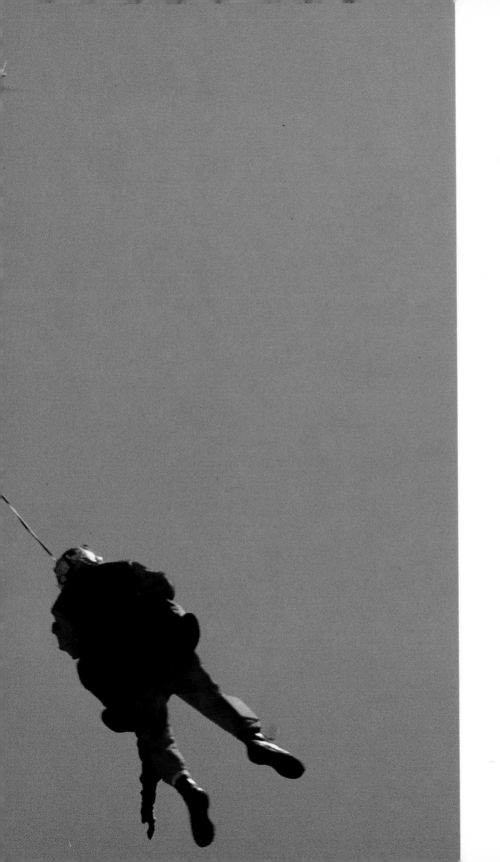

Fallon crew training with a stokes
litter down among the boulders

Above Lemoore crewman rappelling from a Twin Huey. A safety line is attached to his harness. As he rappels down, slack on the safety line is given by the remaining crewman in the helicopter

Right UH-1N from Lemoore NAS about to begin a hoist operation. Rescue helicopters from Lemoore have performed many difficult high mountain rescues in the Yosemite National Park and other areas of the Sierra Nevada Mountains

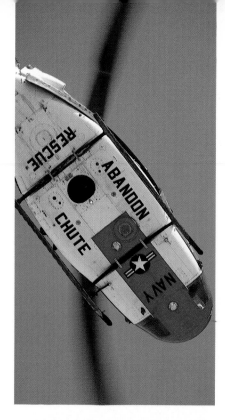

The reminder on the bottom of the helicopter is for military aircrew to get out of their parachute. The rotorwash would inflate it and blow the pilot away from the helicopter

UH-1N from Fallon NAS about to make a one skid landing. This technique is used to load or unload personnel from terrain which is too steep to allow a normal landing. The pilot will make several passes before attempting a landing or coming to a hover. This gives the pilot a chance to gauge the wind speed and direction and spot any obstacles. The training schedule is very rigid for the pilots and crews. Separate 14 day, 30 day, semi-annual, and annual training requirements must be completed in order for the pilot to remain SAR qualified. It usually takes 12 to 18 months to become a SAR command pilot

Left Some of the pilots and crewmen assigned to the rescue unit at Fallon NAS. Sage brush and mountains are typical of the terrain around Fallon. Over 250 miles from the Pacific ocean, the base is used by attack and fighter aircraft for bombing and air combat manoeuvring training

Above The bracket behind the pilot's door on the UH-1N is for a high-power searchlight for night SAR missions. The practice ranges are often active well past midnight and the rescue helicopters must be able to respond to any crashes. Inside the cabin, just in front of the sliding door is a 100 gallon auxiliary fuel bladder. This gives the Twin Huey a total flight time of 2.8 hours. The design on the nose of the helicopter is of a longhorn steer. LONGHORN is the radio call sign of Fallon's rescue helicopters

Canadian Armed Forces

View of a glacier in British Columbia from the observer's window of a de Havilland Canada CC-115 Buffalo. On a search mission over this type of terrain, the Buffalo will follow the contours of the mountains at 500–1500 feet above the ground

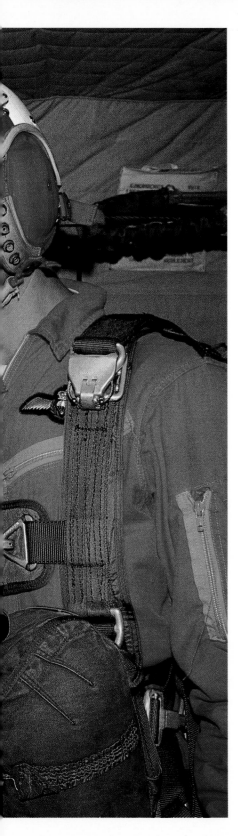

Left Two SAR Techs checking each other's equipment before a parachute jump. SAR Tech's are skilled in scuba diving, mountain rescue and advanced medical techniques in addition to parachuting

Above SAR Tech of No 442 Sqn communicating with the Buffalo pilot on the intercom before a jump. A clearly understood plan of action for the whole crew is essential to an effective, safe jump. Anyone can stop it by a simple command of 'Go around'

SAR Tech at one of the observation
windows in the rear of a CC-115.
The windows bubble out and give
excellent visibility to the sides and
below the Buffalo

Two SAR Techs exiting a CC-115:
the normal drop altitude is 800 feet
above the ground on actual
missions, but 1200 feet is used for
training jumps. Equipment is
dropped between 150–300 feet
AGL

A flight engineer assisting a SAR Tech into his brush suit. This thick nylon jump suit is used for protection when jumping into trees or thick brush

A Buffalo on a dirt strip in British Columbia on an actual rescue mission. The primitive strip was cleared for use by small general aviation aircraft and is only 2400 feet long with tall trees at both ends. The 38,000-pound Buffalo landed in about 1000 feet. As the dirt strip was too narrow for the aircraft to turn around, the pilot put the propellers into reverse pitch and taxied backwards to the end of the runway. Crewmen walked under each wingtip to guide the pilot and warn him of any impending obstructions

The Buffalo at the moment of take-off from the rescue scene. Although the strip is merely loose dirt and has a hump in the middle, the Buffalo still only took about 1200 feet to get airborne

Left Landing gear coming up immediately after take-off. In order to take off safely in case of an engine failure, several people and 3000 pounds of equipment were offloaded from the aircraft

Main picture The Buffalo taking off with the four victims of a light airplane crash safely aboard. Wisps of smoke to the left of the runway mark the crash site (the airplane crashed on take-off). The victims were flown to Vancouver, BC for hospital treatment

Below Although over 20 years old (the aircraft was produced to fulfil a US Army requirement issued to industry in May 1962 and the prototype made its maiden flight on 9 April 1964), the Buffalo performs its SAR role magnificently. It will be difficult to find a replacement that will be able to do the job as well

Left Boeing-Vertol CH-113 Labrador of No 442 Sqn, Canadian Armed Forces, landing next to the fishing camp where the casualties of the light airplane crash were initially taken. A helicopter was despatched in case the site proved inaccessible for the Buffalo

Above This is what is known as a confined area landing. The rail fence to the right of the helicopter is inside the rotor diameter. Loose boards and other debris at the site were also hazards. Because of these and other obstacles, the pilot had to *back* into the landing zone

View from a Labrador of one of the hundreds of glaciers in the Coastal Mountains of British Columbia. Some of these peaks reach 10,000 feet, where the Labrador's performance rapidly deteriorates

All CH-113s recently completed an equipment update. They received new, faster rescue hoists, extra fuel tanks, new auxiliary power units and new radar sets. The CH-113 is a modified version of the CH-46 Sea Knight operated by the US Navy and US Marine Corps

Left The hoist boom pivots to ease the entry of a victim in a stokes litter or other rescue device. Following Canadian regulations, all markings are in both English and French

Above CH-113 of No 442 Sqn on alert at CAF Base Comox in British Columbia. Large red pods carry extra fuel. SAR aircraft may work a mission far offshore one day and a search deep in the Canadian wilderness the next. Canada is divided into four SAR regions with at least one SAR unit located in each

71

SAR Tech rappelling from a Labrador. Note how the pilots can see almost straight down through the chin windows. Black 'nose' houses a search/weather radar. The bracket under the nose is for a powerful searchlight

Main picture A Labrador approaching a landing site on the side of a forested hill. There are many remote camps and settlements in British Columbia which require air evacuation when a person is ill or injured

Inset Shadow of a Labrador during a landing approach at a remote site. The tandem rotor design of the CH-113 is less affected by crosswinds than a normal tail rotor type helicopter. Pilots use this to advantage in confined areas

CH-113 cruising over a glacier on Vancouver Island. Weather conditions and winds can vary greatly over short distances on the mountains

Labrador crew consists of two pilots, two flight engineers (one to operate the hoist), and two SAR Techs. The CH-113 is fitted with extensive communications equipment. The crews can talk to police units, ambulances, ships, aircraft and can even access the telephone company via a mobile telephone frequency. This flight engineer is standing by in the doorway prior to a remote site landing

Below Flight engineer in the doorway keeps the pilot informed of the distance between the ground and the landing gear

Labrador heads back to Comox after performing an impressive touchdown on the glacier

Main picture Labrador touching down on Comox Glacier on Vancouver Island, British Columbia. This is a frequent training area for No 442 Sqn. Landings must be done lightly to make sure the ice doesn't suddenly collapse and roll the helicopter over. The squadron has a fleet of four Buffaloes and five Labradors to cover all of British Columbia and up to 200 miles off its coastline

Right Labrador approaching a
rescue boat to hoist off an SAR
Tech. Note the wall of spray being
pushed ahead of the helicopter

Far right SAR Techs hooking up
to the crane hoist cable on the deck
of a crash rescue boat. Rotorwash
creates a heavy, stinging spray
when working close to the water

Left Labrador directly over the boat in the hoisting position. Rotorwash, spray and noise can create a frightening environment. A SAR Tech is usually lowered to the vessel first to calm and instruct the victims

Above SAR Tech being hoisted down to the deck of a CAF rescue boat assigned to Comox

United States Air Force

Bell HH-1H Huey of the 304th Aerospace Rescue and Recovery Squadron (ARRS) based at Portland, Oregon lowering a jungle penetrator on a hoist practice mission. Note how the hoist boom is mounted externally. This is an unusual arrangement for a Huey, but it makes entry into the cabin easier for anyone on the hoist

Left The crew of the HH-1H from the 304th ARRS is surveying possible landing sites. The 304th was the first Air Force Reserve unit to join the Military Assistance to Safety and Traffic (MAST) programme. Begun in 1978, the unit serves a 22 county area in northern Oregon and southern Washington State

Left The flight engineer, lying on his belly in the cabin, is talking the pilot down onto a riverbed of uneven rocks

Below HH-1H from the 304th ARRS sitting in a dry riverbed in Canada. The unit travels to Canada almost every year to conduct training exercises

Right UH-1N Twin Huey of the
1550th Combat Crew Training
Wing (CCTW) based at Kirtland
AFB, New Mexico with a sling load
over the desert. Missile support
duties require sling loading a
variety of equipment to the widely
scattered silos. The UH-1N can
sling as much as 5000 pounds. In
addition to missile site support, the
Air Force employs the Twin Huey
for SAR, VIP transport and special
operations

Opposite With a full crew of pilot,
copilot, flight engineer and a
pararescueman, the HH-1H has an
endurance of slightly less than two
hours on a normal fuel load. It was
designed as a local base rescue
helicopter to handle crash rescue
duties within short distances of
airfields

Sikorsky HH-3E Jolly Green Giant of the 304th ARRS undergoing repairs on a training exercise at CAFB Comox, British Columbia. On the left are CT-113 Silver Stars (Canadair-built Lockheed T-33s), used as opponents in air combat manoeuvre training for CAF CF-5 and CF-18 Hornet fighters

Preceding pages and main picture HH-3E from the 304th ARRS comes to the hover before lowering its jungle penetrator over a clearing next to a lake. The orange part of the penetrator is a removable float to keep it from sinking out of reach of a survivor in a water rescue. Fifty HH-3Es were converted from CH-3E cargo helicopters in late 1966 and early 1967. They received rescue hoists, armour plating, self-sealing fuel tanks, armament, and the ability to refuel in mid-air from C-130 tankers. The Sikorsky CH-3 and HH-3 series were derived from the highly successful SH-3 naval helicopter. The Air Force versions have a rear cargo ramp for quick loading and unloading of equipment and personnel. During the volcanic eruption of Mt St Helens in Washington State in 1980, the 304th ARRS was credited with saving 66 lives

Inset Flight engineer aboard a CH-3 assigned to the 1550th CCTW. The helicopter is travelling at 100 knots and 100 feet on a low-level training mission

Main picture HH-3E over one of the ranges near Kirtland AFB, which are used to train pilots in tactical operations. The pilot progressing from basic flight training must learn to fly the particular type of helicopter his unit is using as well as how to accomplish tactical missions while at Kirtland

Inset During combat missions, the HH-3E is armed with two 7.62 mm M-60 machine guns that fire out from windows on each side of the helicopter

Sikorsky CH-3E at one of the remote landing sites used to train pilots at
Kirtland. There are over 25 landing sites spread out over the deserts and
mountains that surround the base. Several CH-3s are assigned to Kirtland
and are used to train pilots in all aspects of combat rescue and special
operations, but not air-refuelling

CH-3E making a steep diving bank after take-off from the remote site. Pilots
are taught to use the terrain to mask the helicopter from hostile fire

Opposite page From helicopter to boat: view from the cockpit of a HH-3E as it sits in the waters of the Elephant Butte Reservoir south of Kirtland AFB. All the H-3 series' have watertight hulls. As the rotor brake is applied to stop the blades after they have been disengaged, the torque causes the helicopter to rotate slowly in the water

Left HH-3E hovering as the crew practice a water hoist rescue. The shield over the engine intakes above the cockpit are designed to prevent the ingestion of ice that is thrown off the windscreen

Left Crew of a CH-3E waiting as the helicopter is refuelled at Truth or Consequences, New Mexico. Believe it or not, the town was renamed after a popular game show in the sixties and seventies

Above The imposing nose of a Sikorsky MH-53J Super Jolly Green Giant. This is the latest in combat rescue and special operations helicopters. It has terrain following radar, radar warning receivers and other sophisticated equipment to find downed airmen in darkness and bad weather. Despite a rotor diameter of 72 feet and a gross weight of 42,000 pounds, the Super Jolly Green Giant is amazingly agile. By the end of 1989 it is planned to replace the C model with new MH-53Js. Eventually, all existing C models are expected to be modified to J model standard

HH-53 performing a hoist training mission. The downwash from the rotor blades creates winds of almost 90 mph directly under the helicopter. In addition to remote site landings and low-level flying, advanced manoeuvres designed to defeat missile and fighter attacks are also practised

HH-53 hovering over a lake during the water hoist training. The HH-53
first appeared in late 1967 as the front line combat rescue helicopter in
Vietnam. Powered by a pair of General Electric T64 turboshafts of 3925
shp, the HH-53 can lift a sling load of 20,000 pounds or carry 38 combat-
equipped troops. In medevac configuration, it can accommodate 22 litter
patients and four attendants

Interior view of an HH-53 facing aft. A 7.62 mm Minigun is mounted on the rear cargo ramp to suppress ground fire. The gunner is also used as an extra set of eyes during tactical operations

Cabin of the HH-53 looking forward. The 7.62 mm Minigun swings into the doorway for operation

Opposite page Flight engineer manning a 7.62 mm Minigun in the right-hand door of an HH-53. This gun is capable of firing 4000 rounds per minute. During combat operations, the HH-53 is equipped with three Miniguns, one out each side and one on the rear ramp

Post-flight maintenance on an HH-53: being complex and over twenty years old, the Super Jolly tends to be labour intensive. The HH-53 can carry either two 450 (as here) or 650 US gallon external fuel tanks. These can be jettisoned in an emergency

The landing gear of the CH-53 is kept down at all times on low-level missions in case an emergency landing is necessary. This leaves one less thing to do when the pilots are under pressure

Inset Rear scanner/gunner on the cargo ramp of an HH-53. In order to practise daylight low-level flying, the crew must consist of two pilots and three scanners

Main picture Lockheed HC-130H Hercules of the 304th ARRS going through the 'bird bath' at Comox to wash off salt spray after a low-level mission over the ocean. The nose is configured to mount two fork-like projections to catch the parachute shrouds of a space capsule. They can also catch and reel in a balloon cable attached to a man on the ground—the Fulton Recovery System

Main picture HC-130H flying over Vancouver Island, British Columbia. The hump on the top of the fuselage behind the cockpit contains a radio tracking device which is used to locate returning space capsules. It can also be used for homing in on distress signals on several frequencies. The aircraft has a maximum endurance of 14 hours, and the crew consists of a pilot, copilot, navigator, flight engineer, radio operator, loadmaster and two pararescuemen

Inset HC-130P of the 1550th CCTW trailing two hoses at the beginning of an air-refuelling operation with an HH-3E helicopter. The Hercules slowly overtakes the helicopter and then reduces airspeed

Left HC-130P ready to receive a helicopter. The flaps are set at 70 degrees to slow the aircraft down to within 10 knots of stall speed to allow the helicopter to maintain position. The white bands around the hose indicate the length extended

Above The HH-3E flying in the 'pre-connect' position behind the Hercules. The helicopter is matching the speed of the tanker and getting ready to move forward and make contact with the drogue

Overleaf Contact! The refuelling system allows the Hercules to burn the fuel in the 1800 US gallon cargo bay tank for extra range and the aircraft can also give some of its internal fuel to the helicopter if required

Above Consolidated PBY Catalina amphibian on display at the Rescue
Museum at Kirtland AFB, New Mexico. Before the advent of air-refuelling
for helicopters, the Air Force employed a large number of amphibians

Below Grumman HU-16 Albatross amphibian, a workhorse SAR machine during the Korean and Vietnam Wars

The helicopter display at the Rescue Museum features (left to right) UH-1F, H-21, HH-43 and H-19

Left and overleaf Formation flight over the mountains of British Columbia of aircraft operated by the 304th ARRS based at Portland, Oregon: HC-130H, HH-3E and HH-1H

The rare sight of an HH-3E and HH-1H leading what is possibly a unique line astern formation with the HC-130H bringing up the rear

The 304th ARRS uses both the HH-3E (left) and HH-1H to perform
MAST missions. Although there are civilian medical helicopters in the
304th's area, the hoist and high altitude capabilities of these helicopters are
still unique

Pararescueman starting an intravenous line on another student during eight weeks of intensive medical training. Pararescuemen are also skilled at parachuting, mountain climbing, scuba diving and small arms. They are trained for different skills by schools around the USA. However, the training headquarters are located at Kirtland AFB

Two HH-1Hs, two HH-3Es, an HC-130H and an HC-130P form an impressive line-up at Comox, British Columbia, during a training deployment

Student treating the simulated victim of a light airplane crash at the pararescue training facility at Kirtland AFB